4-9-96

The NORTH POLE® Village Cookbook

SANTA'S FAVORITE RECIPES

Published by
Heritage Yule Trim©, Inc.

ISBN 0-9649423-0-5

Printed in the United States
10 9 8 7 6 5 4 3 2 1

A Shared Evening

In midwinter, long before this Christmas,
Neilan Lund, architect of the North Pole Village
series, invited his friends from Department 56
to gather round an open hearth. As they talked late
into that starry night, they formed a playful idea
and agreed to contact Mrs. Claus and Mrs. Rimpy
the next morning. Yes, it was a stirring possibility!

Immediately these two friends and wonderful
cooks began to work on recipes that would have a
connection to the North Pole Village. Then they
began to weave a whimsical story about their
shared experience, awakening to the childlike magic
of Christmas.

Contents

Chapter 1

Cookies

Santa's Easy Sugar Cookies

Baker Elves' Brown Sugar Cutouts

Beard Barber Poles

Prancer's Peanut Butter Delights

Obbie's Christmas Snowballs

Rimpy's Gingersnaps

Tassy's Toffee Fingers

Blitzen's Brownies

Comet's Cinnamon Logs

Dasher and Dancer's Date Pinwheels

It's Christmas

Santa is so happy this time of year.
All the North Pole is filled with good cheer.
Baker Elves, up to their elbows in dough,
Are getting ready for the year's biggest show.

Santa's Easy Sugar Cookies

1 cup sugar
1 cup butter or regular
  margarine, softened
1 egg
2 cups all-purpose flour

1/2 teaspoon salt
1/2 teaspoon baking soda
1 teaspoon vanilla extract
Colored sugar

Heat oven to 375°. In large bowl, mix sugar and butter with spoon until smooth. Mix in egg. Mix in flour, salt, baking soda and vanilla extract until smooth.

Shape dough by teaspoons into balls. Place about 2 inches apart on ungreased cookie sheet. Flatten with bottom of glass that has been greased and dipped in colored sugar.

Bake 8 to 10 minutes or until light brown around edges.
Makes about 4 dozen cookies.

Mrs. Claus, whose cookies are always the best,
Bakes and decorates for holiday guests.
While the elves sprinkle sugar on her cookie display,
They slyly sample a few, "Just testing," they say.

Baker Elves' Brown Sugar Cutouts

1/2 cup brown sugar
  (packed)
1 cup butter or regular
  margarine, softened
2 1/2 cups all-purpose flour

1/2 teaspoon salt
1/2 teaspoon vanilla
  extract
1/2 cup very finely
  chopped pecans

Heat oven to 300°. In large bowl, mix brown sugar and butter with spoon until smooth. Mix in flour, salt and vanilla extract until blended. Mix in pecans (dough will be stiff).

Divide dough in half. Roll one half about 1/4 inch thick between two sheets of waxed paper. Using a variety of 2-inch Christmas cookie cutters, cut out cookies. Place about 1 inch apart on ungreased cookie sheet. Repeat with other half.

Bake about 25 minutes or until set (cookies will not brown).
Makes about 4 dozen cookies.

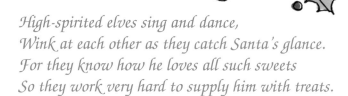

High-spirited elves sing and dance,
Wink at each other as they catch Santa's glance.
For they know how he loves all such sweets
So they work very hard to supply him with treats.

Beard Barber Poles

1 cup powdered sugar
1 cup butter or regular
  margarine, softened
1 egg
1 teaspoon vanilla extract

$1/2$ teaspoon peppermint
  extract
$2^1/2$ cups all-purpose flour
$1/2$ teaspoon salt
$1/2$ teaspoon red food color

Heat oven to 375°. In large bowl, mix powdered sugar and
butter with spoon until smooth. Mix in egg, vanilla extract
and peppermint extract. Mix in flour and salt until blended.
Divide dough in half. Mix red food color into one half (leave
other half plain).

For each pole, take scant teaspoon of red dough and scant
teaspoon of white dough; squeeze together 2 or 3 times until
marbled. Shape into ball, then roll into 4-inch rope. Very
gently twist rope about 3 times to create diagonal stripes of a
barber pole. Place on ungreased cookie sheet. Repeat with
remaining dough.

Bake about 8 minutes or until set.
Makes about 6 dozen cookies.

Prancer's Peanut Butter Delights

1/2 cup granulated sugar
1/2 cup brown sugar
  (packed)
1/2 cup butter or regular
  margarine, softened
1/2 cup peanut butter
1 egg
2 tablespoons milk

1 teaspoon vanilla extract
1 3/4 cups all-purpose
  flour
1 teaspoon baking soda
1/2 teaspoon salt
Granulated sugar
About 48 chocolate kisses
  (unwrapped)

Heat oven to 375°. In large bowl, mix granulated sugar, brown
sugar, butter and peanut butter with spoon until smooth. Mix
in egg, milk and vanilla extract. Mix in flour, baking soda
and salt until blended.

Shape dough into 1-inch balls. Roll in sugar. Place about
2 inches apart on ungreased cookie sheet.

Bake 10 to 12 minutes or until set. Immediately press a
chocolate kiss into each cookie.

Makes about 4 dozen cookies.

Obbie's Christmas Snowballs

1/2 cup powdered sugar
1 cup butter or regular
    margarine, softened
1 teaspoon vanilla extract

13/4 cups all-purpose flour
2/3 cup finely chopped
    pecans
Powdered sugar

Heat oven to 400°. In large bowl, mix powdered sugar, butter and vanilla extract with spoon until smooth. Mix in flour until blended. Mix in pecans.

Shape dough by teaspoons into 1-inch balls. Place about 2 inches apart on ungreased cookie sheet.

Bake about 8 minutes or until set. Immediately roll in powdered sugar. Cool completely. Roll in powdered sugar.
Makes about 4 dozen cookies.

Obbie selects books for Santa's pack,
Favorite stories read front to back;
As he reads in his room above the bookstore,
He samples Snowballs and always wants more!

Rimpy's Gingersnaps

1 cup sugar
1/2 cup shortening
1/4 cup butter or regular
    margarine, softened
1 egg
1/4 cup molasses
2 cups all-purpose flour

1 teaspoon cinnamon
1 teaspoon ginger
1/2 teaspoon cloves
2 teaspoons baking soda
1/4 teaspoon salt
Granulated sugar

In large bowl, mix sugar, shortening and butter with spoon until smooth. Mix in egg and molasses. Mix in flour, cinnamon, ginger, cloves, baking soda and salt until blended. Cover and chill about 1 hour.

Heat oven to 375°. Grease cookie sheet. Shape dough into 1-inch balls. Roll in sugar. Place on cookie sheet.

Bake 10 to 12 minutes or until set.
Makes about 5 dozen cookies.

Rimpy works before dawn, sets dough to shape,
Then creams cookie dough that will later bake
Into spicy Gingersnaps for his North Pole friends.
His bakings and friendship are a wonderful blend.

Tassy's Toffee Fingers

1 cup brown sugar (packed)
1 cup butter or regular
  margarine, softened
1 egg yolk
2 cups all-purpose flour

1/2 teaspoon almond extract
11.5-ounce package milk
  chocolate chips
3/4 cup chopped almonds,
  toasted

Heat oven to 350°. Grease 13x9-inch pan. In large bowl, mix brown sugar and butter with spoon until smooth. Mix in egg yolk. Mix in flour and almond extract until blended. Spread evenly in pan.

Bake about 30 minutes or until light brown. Sprinkle with milk chocolate chips. Return to oven for about 3 minutes or until chocolate is very soft, then spread evenly. Sprinkle with almonds. Cool completely. Cut into 3x1-inch bars.

Makes about 3 dozen cookies.

Tassy and Hassel work night and day
To knit mittens and mufflers for kids who play.
When you make a snowman, ski and ice skate,
You must keep warm, now don't hesitate.

Blitzen's Brownies

4 ounces unsweetened
  chocolate
1 cup butter or regular
  margarine
4 eggs
2 cups sugar
1/2 teaspoon salt

1 1/2 teaspoons vanilla
  extract
1 1/3 cups all-purpose flour
1 cup chopped nuts
1/2 cup raspberry
  preserves
Glaze (below)

In medium saucepan, melt chocolate and butter over low heat. Stir until completely mixed. Let stand until cool.

Heat oven to 350°. Grease 13x9-inch pan. Stir eggs, sugar, salt and vanilla extract into chocolate mixture with spoon until blended. Mix in flour and nuts thoroughly. Spread evenly in pan.

Bake about 30 minutes or until top is dry. Cool completely. Spread with raspberry preserves. Drizzle Glaze from tip of spoon over raspberry preserves. Cut into 2x1-inch bars.

Glaze: Stir together 1 cup powdered sugar and 1 to 2 tablespoons milk.

Makes about 4 dozen brownies.

Comet's Cinnamon Logs

1 cup butter or regular
  margarine, softened
3-ounce package cream
  cheese, softened
1/2 cup sugar

1 teaspoon cinnamon
1 teaspoon vanilla
2 cups all-purpose flour
Cinnamon-sugar

In large bowl, mix butter and cream cheese with spoon until smooth. Mix in sugar, cinnamon and vanilla extract. Mix in flour until blended. Cover and chill about 1 hour.

Heat oven to 375°. Shape dough by teaspoons into 2-inch rolls. Place about 2 inches apart on ungreased cookie sheet. Cut off ends so that cookies will resemble logs.

Bake about 10 minutes or until set. Cool slightly. Roll in cinnamon-sugar.

Makes about 5 dozen cookies.

The reindeer prance, just waiting to fly
From Pole to Pole through the clear, starry sky.
Santa gets a boost into his shiny red sleigh
And all hear him shout, "Up, up and away!"

Dasher and Dancer's Date Pinwheels

8-ounce package pitted
 dates, finely chopped
1/4 cup granulated sugar
1/2 cup water
1/2 cup finely chopped nuts
1 cup brown sugar (packed)
1/2 cup shortening

1 egg
1/2 teaspoon vanilla
 extract
13/4 cups all-purpose flour
1 teaspoon baking powder
1/2 teaspoon baking soda
1/2 teaspoon salt

In small saucepan, cook dates, granulated sugar and water until thick. Stir in nuts. Let stand until cool.

In large bowl, mix brown sugar and shortening with spoon until smooth. Mix in egg and vanilla extract. Mix in flour, baking powder, baking soda and salt until blended.

Divide dough in half. Roll one half into 12x7-inch rectangle between two sheets of waxed paper. Spread half of the date mixture over dough. From long end, roll up as for a jelly roll, using waxed paper to help roll dough. Repeat with other half. Wrap and chill about 4 hours or until firm enough to slice.

Heat oven to 375°. Cut roll into slices about 1/4 inch thick. Place about 2 inches apart on ungreased cookie sheet.

Bake about 10 minutes or until light brown. Cool 1 minute before removing from cookie sheet.

Makes about 8 dozen cookies.

Chapter 2

Candies

Letrinka's Sugar & Spice Nuts

Tin Soldiers' Caramel Corn

Elfie's Honey Peanut Nuggets

Reindeer Chewies

Dolls' Luscious Fudge

Snow-Covered Pine Cones

Letrinka makes candy, everything so sweet,
While elves chop nuts and help to complete
Recipes here that are so easy and quick,
Ready in a moment to be sent with St. Nick.

16

Letrinka's Sugar & Spice Nuts

1/4 cup brown sugar
   (packed)
1 teaspoon cinnamon

3 cups pecan halves
1 egg white

Heat oven to 300°. In small bowl, stir together brown sugar and cinnamon until blended. In large bowl, mix pecans and egg white. Add brown sugar mixture; mix until pecans are thoroughly coated.

Spread in single layer in shallow pan. Bake 30 minutes until crisp, stirring every few minutes. Cool completely.

Makes about 3 cups nuts.

Sugar and spice nuts, just right for the season,
Are a wonderful snack whatever the reason,
Trimming the tree, neighborhood singing,
Wrapping surprises for holiday giving.

Tin Soldiers' Caramel Corn

15 cups popped corn
1 cup brown sugar (packed)
1/2 cup butter or regular
   margarine

1/4 cup corn syrup
1/2 teaspoon salt
1/2 teaspoon baking soda

Heat oven to 200°. Divide popcorn between two 13x9-inch pans. In medium saucepan, heat brown sugar, butter, corn syrup and salt over medium heat until bubbly. Cook 5 minutes longer. Remove from heat. Stir in baking soda (mixture will froth up). Pour over popcorn.

Bake 1 hour, stirring every 15 minutes. Pour into large bowls and continue to stir to keep kernels separated. Cool completely. Store in airtight containers.

Makes 15 cups.

Caramel Corn is delicious with a very sweet crunch,
A North Pole favorite for all to munch.
The Tin Soldiers stir, don't miss a beat,
For kids of all ages love this treat.

Elfie's Honey Peanut Nuggets

6-ounce package semisweet
   chocolate chips
6-ounce package
   butterscotch chips

6-ounce package peanut
   butter chips
2 cups honey-roasted
   peanuts

Cover cookie sheet with waxed paper. In medium saucepan,
melt chocolate chips, butterscotch chips and peanut butter
chips over low heat, stirring frequently until smooth.
Remove from heat. Stir in peanuts.

Drop from spoon onto cookie sheet. Chill until firm.
Makes about 4 dozen candies.

Elfie spends the day making skates and sleds
He sharpens and polishes in a near-by shed.
Then he hastens home to a warm crackling fire
For nuggets and tea before time to retire.

Reindeer Chewies

8 ounces white chocolate-
flavored candy coating

3 cups chow mein noodles

Cover cookie sheet with waxed paper. In medium saucepan,
melt candy coating over low heat, stirring frequently until
smooth. Remove from heat. Add chow mein noodles; stir
until thoroughly coated.

Drop from spoon onto cookie sheet. Chill until firm.
Makes about 30 candies.

Reindeer who live in the North Pole Barn
Always enjoy a well-told yarn
About their team, their sleigh and flight
As they prance and dance on Christmas night.

Dolls' Luscious Fudge

11.5-ounce package milk
   chocolate chips
2 cups miniature
   marshmallows

3/4 cup coarsely chopped
   nuts

Butter 8-inch square pan. In medium saucepan, melt
chocolate chips over low heat, stirring frequently. Remove
from heat. Beat until smooth. Stir in marshmallows and nuts.

Spread in pan. Chill until firm. Cut into 1-inch squares.
Makes 64 candies.

Delicious chocolate fudge is the favorite of all
To share with North Pole Villagers, large and small.
Wrap in a box, tie red ribbon tight,
Then give to your friends and see their delight.

Snow-Covered Pine Cones

7-ounce milk chocolate bar
1 teaspoon shortening
About 30 large
  marshmallows

Flaked coconut or finely
  chopped nuts

Cover cookie sheet with waxed paper. In small saucepan, melt chocolate bar and shortening over low heat, stirring frequently until smooth. Cool slightly.

Place a toothpick in each marshmallow. Dip marshmallow into melted chocolate. (Let excess chocolate drip into saucepan.) Roll in coconut. Place on cookie sheet. Chill about 15 minutes or until chocolate has set. Remove toothpicks.

Makes about 30 marshmallow candies.

The kitchens are warm in their Village homes
As girls and boys make candy Pine Cones.
These easy recipes are just right for kids.
"Look, Mom and Dad, look what I did!"

Chapter 3

Breads

Rimpy's Pumpkin Wreath

Neenee's Lingonberry Scones

Orly's Cranberry-Orange Loaf

Bear's Gingerbread

Hassel's Mincemeat Muffins

North Pole Toast

Rimpy's Bakery is a gathering place
For coffee and breads from the glass showcase.
In an old brick oven, breads bake to perfection
Turning out loaves of the very best selection.

Rimpy's Pumpkin Wreath

3 cups sugar
1 cup vegetable oil
3 eggs
16-ounce can pumpkin
3 cups all-purpose flour
1 teaspoon baking soda
1/2 teaspoon salt
1/2 teaspoon baking powder
1 teaspoon cinnamon
1 teaspoon nutmeg
1 teaspoon cloves
1/2 teaspoon allspice
1/2 cup chopped walnuts

Heat oven to 350°. Grease and flour 10-inch bundt cake pan. In large bowl, mix sugar and oil with spoon until smooth. Beat in eggs and pumpkin until blended. Mix in remaining ingredients thoroughly. Pour into pan; spread evenly.

Bake about 1 1/4 hours or until loaf tests done (test with a toothpick). Cool 20 minutes, then remove from pan. Cool completely. If you like, serve with honey butter.

North Pole Note: No bundt cake pan?
Use a 10-inch angel food pan instead.
Makes 1 round loaf.

The wreath above the bakery's red door
Is a special wreath like the bread in this store.
With its cinnamon and nutmeg, Christmas spices,
It fills the air with an aroma that entices.

Neenee's Lingonberry Scones

2 cups all-purpose flour
1/4 cup sugar
2 teaspoons baking powder
1/2 teaspoon baking soda
1/2 teaspoon salt
1/2 cup firm butter or
   regular margarine, cut up

1/3 cup frozen loosely
   packed lingonberries
1 egg
3/4 cup buttermilk
Milk
Sugar

Heat oven to 400°. In large bowl, stir together flour, sugar, baking powder, baking soda and salt. Cut in firm butter until mixture is crumbly. Stir in frozen lingonberries.

In small bowl, beat egg and buttermilk with fork until blended. Stir into flour mixture just until soft dough forms. (Dough will be soft and sticky.)

Turn dough onto floured surface. Knead 10 times, adding flour if necessary. Roll dough 1/2 inch thick. Cut into 2-inch rounds with floured cutter. Place about 2 inches apart on ungreased cookie sheet. Brush tops with milk and sprinkle with sugar.

Bake about 15 minutes or until golden brown. Serve warm.

North Pole Note: You can use fresh or frozen cranberries, halved, if lingonberries are not available.

Makes about 20 scones.

Orly's Cranberry-Orange Loaf

2 cups all-purpose flour
2/3 cup sugar
1 1/2 teaspoons baking
 powder
1/2 teaspoon baking soda
1/2 teaspoon salt
1 egg
3 tablespoons vegetable oil

1 tablespoon grated orange
 peel
3/4 cup orange juice
1 1/3 cups fresh or frozen
 cranberries, chopped
1/2 cup chopped nuts
Orange Glaze (below)

Heat oven to 350°. Grease bottom only of 9x5-inch loaf pan.
In large bowl, stir together flour, sugar, baking powder,
baking soda and salt.

In small bowl, beat egg, oil, orange peel and orange juice
slightly with fork. Stir into flour mixture just until
moistened. Fold in cranberries and nuts. Spread in pan.

Bake about 1 hour or until loaf tests done (test with a
toothpick). Cool 10 minutes, then remove from pan. Cool
completely on wire rack. Drizzle Orange Glaze in zigzag lines
over loaf.

Orange Glaze: Stir together 1/2 cup powdered sugar and
2 teaspoons orange juice.

Makes 1 loaf.

Bear's Gingerbread

1 1/2 cups all-purpose flour
1/4 cup brown sugar
(packed)
1/2 teaspoon salt
1/2 teaspoon baking soda
1 teaspoon ginger

1/2 teaspoon cinnamon
1/2 cup milk
1/4 cup molasses
1/4 cup shortening
1 egg
Streusel Topping (below)

Heat oven to 350°. Grease 8-inch square pan. In large bowl, stir together all ingredients except Topping with spoon. Beat vigorously 1/2 minute or until blended. Spread in pan. Sprinkle evenly with Streusel Topping.

Bake about 30 minutes or until gingerbread tests done (test with a toothpick).

Streusel Topping: Mix 1 tablespoon firm butter or regular margarine, 1/4 cup brown sugar (packed) and 1/4 cup chopped pecans.
Makes 1 square.

Hassel's Mincemeat Muffins

1/2 cup shortening	2 cups all-purpose flour
1/3 cup sugar	3 teaspoons baking powder
1 egg	1 teaspoon salt
1 cup milk	1/2 cup mincemeat

Heat oven to 400°. Line 12 medium muffin cups with paper liners. In large bowl, beat shortening and sugar with spoon until smooth. Stir in egg and milk. Mix in flour, baking powder and salt until blended. Stir in mincemeat. Divide evenly among muffin cups.

Bake about 25 minutes or until muffins test done (test with a toothpick). Immediately remove from cups.

Makes 12 muffins.

Warm and welcoming, Hassel can't resist
These delicious muffins with a mincemeat twist.
Serve hot from the oven on a snowy day
Round your hearth when friends come to stay.

North Pole Toast

3/4 cup sugar
1/2 cup butter or regular
  margarine, softened
1 egg
2 cups all-purpose flour

1/2 teaspoon baking soda
1/4 teaspoon salt
1/2 teaspoon cardamom
1/4 teaspoon nutmeg
1/2 cup buttermilk

Heat oven to 350°. Lightly grease 9x5-inch loaf pan. In large bowl, cream sugar and butter with spoon until light. Beat in egg. Stir in dry ingredients alternately with the buttermilk just until moistened. (Dough will be very stiff.) Spread in pan.

Bake 35 to 40 minutes or until loaf tests done (test with a toothpick). Cool 5 minutes. Run knife around edges of pan, then remove loaf from pan. *Cool completely* on wire rack.

Heat oven to 350°. Grease cookie sheet. Cut cooled loaf into 1/2-inch slices. Place slices on cookie sheet. Bake 10 minutes; turn slices over. Bake 10 minutes more. Cool completely on wire rack. Store in an airtight container.

Makes 1 loaf (about 18 slices toast).

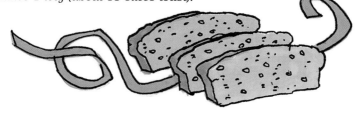

Chapter 4

Gifts

Elfin Gift Baskets

Cupid's Chocolate Sauce

North Pole Caramel Sauce

The Uncommon Gift

Merry Christmas Gatherings

Dear Santa Letter

Elves with great strength in spite of their size
Load Santa's sleigh with gifts that surprise
Like sleds and skis, dolls and drums.
With a holler and shout, liftoff comes.

Elfin Gift Baskets

Everyone loves a surprise. Making a gift for someone in your family or neighborhood is great fun, too.

Here are some delightful ideas to share. Santa's Elves are scampering about with all their Christmas preparations. One might just be peeping over your shoulder as you work.

Line a basket with a Christmas napkin. Add a small breadboard and a favorite nut bread. Scoop out an orange and fill the shell with orange butter. Mound honey nut cream cheese into a lemon shell. Wrap and tie with red yarn.

Tea and cookies invite a moment of joy. Arrange and wrap an assortment of your freshly baked cookies on a Christmas plate. Add a flavorful blend of spicy or calming tea in a colorful container. Take time to linger and enjoy.

Look for unusual glass dishes or wooden boxes during the year. Line with colorful tissue and fill with individually wrapped homemade candies.

Cupid's Chocolate Sauce

1 cup sugar
$1/2$ cup unsweetened cocoa
$1/2$ cup milk

2 tablespoons corn syrup
1 teaspoon vanilla extract

In medium saucepan, mix sugar, cocoa, milk and corn syrup.
Cook over low heat until mixture boils, stirring constantly.
Remove from heat. Stir in vanilla extract. Serve over ice
cream or yogurt. Store any leftover sauce in the refrigerator.

Reheat desired amount in a microwave oven or over low heat
on top of stove.

North Pole Note: Pour Cupid's Chocolate Sauce into glass jar.
Cover the lid with a Christmas needlepoint or cross-stitch
design. Or simply tie with a festive ribbon.
Makes about $1 1/2$ cups sauce.

Cupid, who is one of Santa's reindeer,
Gives Chocolate Sauce as his gift this year.
What could be better than this rich treasure
So easy to make, a delicious pleasure.

North Pole Caramel Sauce

1 cup brown sugar (packed)	3 tablespoons butter or
1/2 cup corn syrup	regular margarine
	1/2 cup half-and-half

In medium saucepan, mix brown sugar, corn syrup and butter. Cook over medium-low heat until mixture boils, stirring constantly. Remove from heat. Gradually stir in half-and-half. Serve with North Pole Pumpkin Pie. Store any leftover sauce in the refrigerator.

Makes about 1 1/3 cups sauce.

Caramel Sauce has a golden touch
Poured into glass jars, a gift loved much.
Drizzle over fruit like an apple or pear,
Serve with Pumpkin Pie for casual flair.

39

The Uncommon Gift

There is warmth and joy in receiving the gift of someone's time. In our busy world it is a precious and uncommon gift wrapped in understanding.

The suggestions here may help you connect with family and friends as you give of yourself.

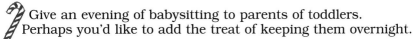

Give an evening of babysitting to parents of toddlers. Perhaps you'd like to add the treat of keeping them overnight.

Draw a snowflake design for snow shoveling and give to a neighbor. Be sure to include your phone number and the times you are available.

Send coupons for long distance phone visits to a relative. Include times that are best for reaching you at home.

Collect photos of your family. Then make a calendar for the home of each family member. Everyone will enjoy the large photos wherever the calendar is hung.

Enjoy a museum exhibit of art, science or natural history with someone who loves to explore.

Merry Christmas Gatherings

What a generous gift of Christmas spirit goes into planning a holiday gathering. Consider time and budget. Be at ease with yourself and enjoy the moment of your own party.

Arrange a sleigh ride or hayride for a small group. It is fun to include all ages. Perhaps you know a storyteller or a banjo player to invite. Remember the hot cider and popcorn.

Invite friends to a dessert buffet. Ask them to share a favorite winter story or poem.

In the fall, reserve a block of tickets for a holiday concert or play, then ask a group to your home for a pretheater dinner. Make it potluck—for the tickets, too.

Treat your children or grandchildren or a neighborhood child to breakfast with Santa. Their eyes will light up and so will the eyes of their busy parents.

Gather family or friends together to make simple decorations like frosted cranberries and popcorn strings. Trim your Christmas tree or lace through evergreen boughs for an easy table decoration.

Choose a group of friends to work together to prepare food several times during the year at a homeless shelter. You'll share the Christmas spirit throughout the coming year.

Dear Santa Letter

Santa Claus
Number One Reindeer Road
North Pole 00001-0001

Dear Santa,

How are you? Are your reindeer ready for Christmas?

I've really been good this year. Have you seen me from your Lookout Tower? I've even played with my sister Sarah.

Do your elves have all the toys made? I've been working really hard on my list. I finally decided on a soccer ball, ice skates and a space game.

My sister can't write yet. She's too little. She wants me to ask you for some clothes to play make-believe and a tricycle with a horn.

Can you carry all that down our chimney?

We'll be baking cookies for your visit.

Love,

MICHAEL   SARAH

Chapter 5

Merry Christmas Dinner

Hot Holiday Cider

Cookie Cutter Canapés

Santa's Stuffed Turkey
or
Elves' Turkey Breast

Snowy Mashed Potatoes

Vixen's Vegetables

Red and Green Salad

Donder's Cranberry Salad

North Pole Pumpkin Pie

Tray of Christmas Cookies and Candies

Santa's Christmas Dinner is traditional fare
Served by the elves for all to share.
Mrs. Claus lined the table with boughs of green
So festive, so bright, a lovely scene.

Hot Holiday Cider

2 quarts apple cider
1 cup orange juice
1/4 cup brown sugar
  (packed)

10 whole cloves
10 whole allspice
4 cinnamon sticks

In large saucepan, heat all ingredients to simmering, stirring until sugar is dissolved. Simmer 10 minutes. Remove cloves, allspice and cinnamon sticks. Serve warm.

Makes 20 servings.

Cookie Cutter Canapés

12 slices white bread
3-ounce package cream
  cheese, softened
1/2 cup finely chopped
  pimiento-stuffed olives

Toppings (squares of green
  and red peppers, thinly
  sliced cucumber, thinly
  sliced radishes, broccoli
  flowerets, herb sprigs)

Cut bread into Christmas shapes, using a variety of 2-inch cookie cutters.

In small bowl, mix cream cheese and olives. Spread over bread cutouts. Decorate with Toppings.

Makes about 2 dozen canapés.

Santa's Stuffed Turkey

12-pound ready-to-cook turkey
1 cup finely chopped celery
1/2 cup butter or regular margarine

1 cup chopped tart apple
14-ounce package sage and onion stuffing mix
2 1/2 cups hot water

Heat oven to 325°. Rinse turkey inside and out with cold water. Drain and pat dry.

In large skillet, cook celery in butter until almost tender, stirring occasionally. Stir in apple. Continue cooking until celery and apple are soft (apple should not be mushy). Empty stuffing mix into large bowl. Add celery-apple mixture. Stir in hot water.

Fill neck and body cavities lightly with stuffing. Close cavities with skewers. Place turkey, breast side up, on a rack in roasting pan. Brush turkey with butter and sprinkle generously with salt and pepper if you like. Do not add water and do not cover pan.

Roast 4 to 4 1/2 hours or until the thigh juices run clear and the drumstick moves easily up and down. (If turkey begins to brown too much, cover loosely with aluminum foil.) Let stand about 30 minutes before carving.

North Pole Note: If there is any stuffing left after filling the turkey, place in a greased casserole. Cover and bake the last 45 minutes with the turkey.

Elves' Turkey Breast

For a smaller gathering of family or friends, roast a turkey breast instead of a whole bird.

Heat oven to 325°. Place a 4-pound turkey breast in shallow pan. Roast uncovered 2 to 2½ hours or until the juices run clear. About 45 minutes before end of roasting time, spoon stuffing into a greased casserole. Cover and place in oven to heat through while turkey continues to cook.

Snowy Mashed Potatoes

3 pounds potatoes, peeled
 and quartered
About ½ cup milk

¼ cup butter or regular
 margarine
1 teaspoon salt

In large saucepan, cook potatoes about 20 minutes or until tender. Drain thoroughly. Mash potatoes, gradually adding milk until potatoes are fluffy. Beat in butter and salt. Sprinkle with chopped parsley or chives if you like.

Makes 8 servings.

Vixen's Vegetables

16-ounce package frozen
  peas
1/4 cup quick-mixing flour
1/4 cup butter or regular
  margarine
1/2 teaspoon salt

1/4 teaspoon pepper
2 cups milk
16-ounce jar whole onions,
  drained
Seasoned Crumbs (below)

Heat oven to 325°. Cook peas as package directs; drain. In medium saucepan, heat flour, butter, salt, pepper and milk to boiling, stirring constantly. Boil and stir 1 minute.

In large bowl, mix sauce, peas and onions. Pour into 2-quart casserole. Sprinkle vegetables with Seasoned Crumbs.

Bake uncovered about 30 minutes or until mixture is bubbly.

Seasoned Crumbs: Mix 1/4 cup dry bread crumbs and 2 teaspoons butter or regular margarine.
Makes 8 servings.

Dinner is enjoyment of conversation and food
With bright colors and textures, a merry mood.
Warmth and laughter fill the air
When stories are retold that can't compare.

Red and Green Salad

1 pint cherry tomatoes
2 cups broccoli flowerets
1 red onion, coarsely
  chopped

1 green pepper, cut into
  pieces
1/2 cup mayonnaise
1/4 cup sugar
2 tablespoons vinegar

In large bowl, mix tomatoes, broccoli, onion and green pepper.
In small bowl, mix mayonnaise, sugar and vinegar. Pour
dressing over vegetables; toss gently. Chill 3 hours to blend
flavors. Toss again just before serving.

Makes 8 servings.

Donder's Cranberry Salad

1 cup boiling water
3-ounce package cranberry-
  flavored gelatin
16-ounce can whole
  cranberry sauce

81/4-ounce can crushed
  pineapple, drained
1 red apple, diced
1/2 cup chopped walnuts

In medium bowl, stir boiling water into gelatin. Stir 2
minutes or until gelatin is completely dissolved. Stir in
cranberry sauce and pineapple. Chill until slightly set.

Stir in apple and walnuts. Pour into 6-cup mold. Chill until
firm. Unmold just before serving.

Makes 8 servings.

North Pole Pumpkin Pie

1 1/2 cups graham cracker crumbs
3 tablespoons granulated sugar
1/4 cup butter or regular margarine, melted
1 cup whipping cream
1 cup canned pumpkin

1/2 cup brown sugar (packed)
1/2 teaspoon ginger
1/4 teaspoon cinnamon
1/4 teaspoon nutmeg
1/2 cup chopped pecans
1 pint butter pecan ice cream, softened

Heat oven to 350°. In small bowl, stir together graham cracker crumbs, granulated sugar and butter. Press in 9-inch pie plate. Bake 10 minutes. Cool completely.

In chilled bowl, beat whipping cream until stiff. In medium bowl, mix pumpkin, brown sugar, ginger, cinnamon, nutmeg and pecans. Fold into whipped cream.

Spoon ice cream into graham cracker crust. Spread pumpkin mixture over ice cream. Freeze until firm. Remove from freezer a few minutes before serving. If you like, serve with North Pole Caramel Sauce.

Makes 8 servings.

Tray of Christmas Cookies and Candies

Christmas invites a childlike smile
To crinkle round the eyes of all for awhile.
So share another cookie, a candy or two,
Made from recipes handed down, grandmother to you.

Christmas is a time to relate and connect
With Santa and the North Pole and all it reflects.
So tie on your skates, feel a sense of worth
That breaks into a smile, fills your heart with mirth.

Santa and all the North Pole Villagers
wish you a very Merry Christmas!

Index

Index

Index

Index

The designs in this book are brought to life in Department 56, Inc.'s North Pole© Series of handcrafted, lighted porcelain houses, buildings and coordinated accessories, sculpted from original drawings by master architect Neilan Lund.

For more information about the North Pole© and the entire Heritage Village Collection® of fine quality porcelain collectibles, or to find the Department 56, Inc. authorized village dealer nearest you, contact:

Department 56 ®
INC.

ONE VILLAGE PLACE
6436 CITY WEST PARKWAY
EDEN PRAIRIE, MN 55344

1-800-LIT-TOWN